BY KATHRYN WALTON

VISIT AMERICA'S NATIONAL PARKS!

VISIT

GRAND CANYON NATIONAL PARK!

Enslow
PUBLISHING

Please visit our website, www.enslow.com. For a free color catalog of all our high-quality books, call toll free 1-800-398-2504 or fax 1-877-980-4454.

Library of Congress Cataloging-in-Publication Data

Names: Walton, Kathryn, 1993- author.
Title: Visit Grand Canyon National Park! / Kathryn Walton.
Description: Buffalo, NY : Enslow Publishing, [2025] | Series: Visit America's national parks! | Includes bibliographical references and index.
Identifiers: LCCN 2024004346 (print) | LCCN 2024004347 (ebook) | ISBN 9781978540606 (library binding) | ISBN 9781978540590 (paperback) | ISBN 9781978540613 (ebook)
Subjects: LCSH: Grand Canyon (Ariz.)–Description and travel–Juvenile literature.
Classification: LCC F788 .W24 2025 (print) | LCC F788 (ebook) | DDC 917.91/3204–dc23/eng/20240213
LC record available at https://lccn.loc.gov/2024004346
LC ebook record available at https://lccn.loc.gov/2024004347

Published in 2025 by
Enslow Publishing
2544 Clinton Street
Buffalo, NY 14224

Portions of this work were originally authored by Santana Hunt and published as *Grand Canyon National Park*. All new material in this edition is authored by Kathryn Walton.

Copyright © 2025 Enslow Publishing

Designer: Tanya Dellaccio Keeney
Editor: Natalie Humphrey

Photo credits: Series Art (illustration) khezy licious/Shutterstock.com; cover (photo) Amanda Mohler/Shutterstock.com; p. 5 Rainer Lesniewski/Shutterstock.com; p. 7 (top) Sean Pavone/Shutterstock.com; p. 7 (bottom) Pat Tr/Shutterstock.com; p. 9 (top) Sydneymills/Shutterstock.com; p. 9 (bottom) 4kclips/Shutterstock.com; p. 11 Sean Pavone/Shutterstock.com; p. 13 Nikolas_jkd/Shutterstock.com; p. 15 Roman Khomlyak/Shutterstock.com; p. 17 Jim Mallouk/Shutterstock.com; p. 19 (top) Lukas Uher/Shutterstock.com; p. 19 (bottom) Jane Rix/Shutterstock.com.

All rights reserved. No part of this book may be reproduced in any form without permission in writing from the publisher, except by a reviewer.

Some of the images in this book illustrate individuals who are models. The depictions do not imply actual situations or events.

Printed in the United States of America

CPSIA compliance information: Batch #CSENS25: For further information contact Enslow Publishing at 1-800-398-2504.

CONTENTS

WELCOME TO GRAND CANYON NATIONAL PARK!	4
CREATING THE CANYON	6
THE PEOPLE OF THE GRAND CANYON	8
MAKING A NATIONAL PARK	10
HIKING THE RIMS	12
MULES IN THE GRAND CANYON	14
RAFTING THE RIVER	16
OUTSIDE THE CANYON	18
PLANNING YOUR VISIT	20
GLOSSARY	22
FOR MORE INFORMATION	23
INDEX	24

Words in the glossary appear in **bold** type the first time they are used in the text.

WELCOME TO GRAND CANYON NATIONAL PARK!

Grand **Canyon** National Park is the one of the most visited national parks in the United States, and you won't want to miss it! At 1,904 square miles (4,931 sq km), the park has plenty to see and do for anyone who wants an outdoor adventure.

With colorful rock layers and the rushing Colorado River, the Grand Canyon is one of the greatest natural wonders in the world.

| | GRAND CANYON NATIONAL PARK |

ARIZONA

MORE TO KNOW
The Grand Canyon is 277 miles (446 km) long and about 6,000 feet (1,829 m) deep at its lowest point.

Grand Canyon National Park is in northwestern Arizona.

CREATING THE CANYON

The Colorado River created the Grand Canyon. The river was able to carve such a deep and steeply sided canyon because it moves very fast and has a great volume of water.

In addition, the river's mud, sand, and stone caused the canyon rock to **erode** further. Rain, water, and big shifts in **temperature** also helped form the Grand Canyon. It took millions of years for the Grand Canyon to look the way it does today.

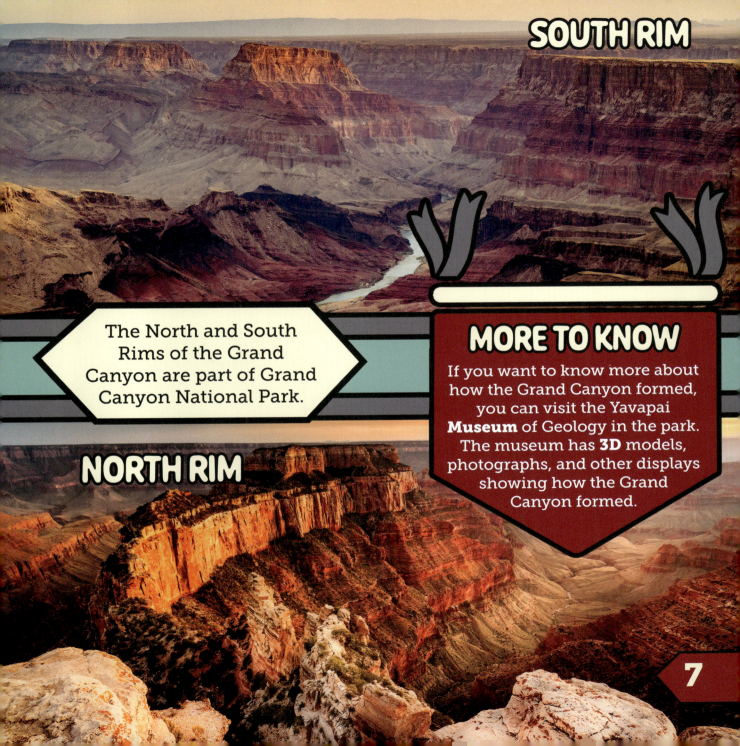

SOUTH RIM

NORTH RIM

The North and South Rims of the Grand Canyon are part of Grand Canyon National Park.

MORE TO KNOW

If you want to know more about how the Grand Canyon formed, you can visit the Yavapai **Museum** of Geology in the park. The museum has **3D** models, photographs, and other displays showing how the Grand Canyon formed.

7

THE PEOPLE OF THE GRAND CANYON

People have lived in the Grand Canyon for over 12,000 years! Places where the first people in the Americas lived have been found in the Grand Canyon. Many different Native American groups starting forming villages there around 500 CE.

Native Americans still live in the Grand Canyon area today. The Navajo, Havasupai, and Hualapai **reservations** are open to visitors. Through tours of their land, visitors can learn the history of the people who lived in the Grand Canyon long before it was part of the United States.

Archaeologists studying the Grand Canyon have found pots, tools, broken pottery, and other items from early Native peoples.

MORE TO KNOW

The Hualapai Nation still manages the Grand Canyon West, sometimes called the West Rim. The Havasu Falls area is owned by the Havasupai people.

GRAND CANYON
West
Land of the Hualapai Nation
GAMYU

MAKING A NATIONAL PARK

In 1893, President Benjamin Harrison set up the Grand Canyon Forest Reserve. In 1919, that part of the Grand Canyon area became a national park, after Arizona became a state in 1912.

Grand Canyon National Park as it is today was formed in 1975, when Marble Canyon National Monument became part of the park. Other lands protected by the U.S. government were added too. Grand Canyon National Park today starts where Arizona meets Utah and stretches to the Grand Wash Cliffs.

The Desert View Watchertower was built in 1932. Visitors can take in the view from the upper floors!

MORE TO KNOW

Grand Canyon National Park doesn't just protect nature. It also protects the history of the people who lived in the park long ago.

HIKING THE RIMS

Grand Canyon National Park is a great place to hike! There are many miles of hiking trails around and down into the canyon.

Those who are especially adventurous can even hike across the Grand Canyon! There's a trail that connects the South Rim to the North Rim. You have to climb down one side of the canyon and up the other! If you choose to travel around the canyon, it's about 220 miles (354 km) from the South Rim to the North Rim.

MORE TO KNOW
If you don't want to hike, there's a shuttle that will take you from one side of the Grand Canyon to the other.

During the summer, it's best to hike early in the morning or after 4 p.m. to beat the heat!

13

MULES IN THE GRAND CANYON

Have you ever wanted to ride a mule? One of the most popular ways to see the Grand Canyon is by mule. Some rides are only a few hours. Others take riders to the bottoms of the canyon to stay overnight at Phantom Ranch.

Hiking and riding in the park can cause problems for people who have heart or breathing problems. The air is thin at higher **elevations**. This can make it harder to take part in activities like hiking.

MORE TO KNOW
The North Rim is higher than the South Rim at 8,000 feet (2,438 m) above sea level. The South Rim is about 7,000 feet (2,134 m) above sea level.

If mules and hikes aren't for you, you can rent a bike to ride through Grand Canyon National Park!

15

RAFTING THE RIVER

Rafting on the Colorado River is another popular way to see the Grand Canyon. Rafting trips can be three days to three weeks long. Some of these trips take travelers through **white water**. "Smooth water" trips are through calmer parts of the river.

When on a rafting trip on the Colorado River, you may have to carry all your food and water. If you're going on a longer trip, you may need to carry your own toilet as well!

MORE TO KNOW

Most rafting trips have a guide to take you through the river. With the right permission and **experience**, though, you can raft down the Colorado River alone!

The Colorado River flows through Colorado, Utah, Arizona, Nevada, and California.

OUTSIDE THE CANYON

There's more to Grand Canyon National Park than just the main canyon! Forests, side canyons, and the nearby **plateau** are all must-see stops on your Grand Canyon adventure. Try to spot a California condor or bald eagle flying through the sky and enjoy the more than 1,500 kinds of plants and trees in the park.

Kaibab National Forest surrounds much of the park. Lake Mead isn't far away. Zion National Park is only around 100 miles (161 km) away.

The walls of the Grand Canyon are layered in pink, gray, purple, and many shades of brown.

MORE TO KNOW

If you visit the Grand Canyon, make sure to stop by the Painted Desert nearby and see the colorful rocks.

GRAND CANYON NATIONAL PARK

NATIONAL PARK SERVICE

PLANNING YOUR VISIT

It's important to pick the right time for your visit to the Grand Canyon. While the South Rim is open year-round, the North Rim is closed from December to May. Most people visit Grand Canyon National Park from March to October.

No matter what time of year you visit, if you plan to hike, make sure to bring everything you need with you! Remember to pack water, food, and other supplies. The Grand Canyon can be dangerous if you aren't prepared.

MORE TO KNOW
Most people visiting the Grand Canyon National Park enter through the South Rim.

GRAND CANYON NATIONAL PARK

THE FACTS

ESTABLISHED
1919

SIZE
1,904 square miles (4,931 sq km)

NUMBER OF VISITORS EACH YEAR
Nearly 5 million

NATIVE WILDLIFE
foxes, bald eagles, coyotes, peregrine falcons, and more

NATIVE PLANTS
cactus, yucca, and cottonwoods in the canyon; pine, scrub oak, and sagebrush on the rim

MUST-SEE STOPS
the Colorado River, North and South Rims, and Mather Point

GLOSSARY

archaeologist: Someone who studies the tools and other objects left behind by ancient people.

canyon: A deep valley with steep sides.

elevation: Height above sea level.

erode: To wear away outer layers of rock or soil by the action of wind and water.

experience: To have gained skills doing something.

museum: A building in which things of interest are displayed.

plateau: A large area of land with raised sides and a level top.

rafting: Traveling in a flat boat with low sides.

reservation: Land set aside by the U.S. government for Native Americans.

temperature: How hot or cold something is.

3D: Something that is made to be in three dimensional form.

white water: Water that is fast moving, white, and foamy.

FOR YOUR INFORMATION

Books

Frisch, Nate. *Grand Canyon National Park*. Mankato, MN: Creative Education and Creative Paperbacks, 2025.

Jacobson, Bray. *The Grand Canyon*. Buffalo, NY: Gareth Stevens Publishing, 2023.

Websites

National Geographic Kids: Grand Canyon National Park
kids.nationalgeographic.com/nature/article/grand-canyon
Learn more about the history of the Grand Canyon National Park.

National Park Service: Grand Canyon
www.nps.gov/grca/learn/kidsyouth/index.htm
Find out what you can do on your trip to the Grand Canyon.

Publisher's note to educators and parents: Our editors have carefully reviewed these websites to ensure that they are suitable for students. Many websites change frequently, however, and we cannot guarantee that a site's future contents will continue to meet our high standards of quality and educational value. Be advised that students should be closely supervised whenever they access the internet.

INDEX

Arizona, 5, 10, 17

Colorado River, 4, 6, 16, 17, 21

Desert View Watchtower, 11

Grand Canyon Forest Reserve, 10

Grand Canyon West (West Rim), 9

Grand Wash Cliffs, 10

Havasu Falls, 9

Havasupai, 8, 9

hike, 12, 13, 14, 15, 20

Hualapai, 8, 9

Kaibab National Forest, 18

mules, 14, 15

Navajo, 8

North Rim, 7, 12, 15, 20, 21

Painted Desert, 19

Phantom Ranch, 14

rafting, 16

size, 4, 5, 21

South Rim, 8, 12, 15, 20, 21

Utah, 10, 17

Yavapai Museum of Geology, 7